S
Memory
MAP
For Girls

A CREATIVE JOURNAL

BARBOUR BOOKS
An Imprint of Barbour Publishing, Inc.

Published by Barbour Books, an imprint of Barbour Publishing, Inc., 1810 Barbour Drive, Uhrichsville, Ohio 44683, www.barbourbooks.com

Our mission is to inspire the world with the life-changing message of the Bible.

Member of the
Evangelical Christian
Publishers Association

Printed in China.

06528   0719   DS

What Does Scripture Memory Look Like?

Get ready to hide the truths of God's Word in your heart with this creative journal, where every colorful page will guide you to create your very own scripture memory map—by writing out specific goals, thoughts, and ideas that you can follow from start to finish—as you begin your Bible memory verse journey. (Be sure to record the date on each one of your scripture memory maps so you can look back over time and track what you've learned!)

The Scripture Memory Map for Girls not only will encourage you to know the truths of God's Word even better but also will help you build a healthy spiritual habit of Bible memorization for life!

Don't know where to begin? Check out the helpful list of recommended Bible memory verses at the back of this book!

Date:

MY MEMORY VERSE FOR TODAY:

....

....

....

....

....

This verse is important to remember because. . .

....

....

....

....

....

WHAT IT MEANS TO MY FAITH:

....

....

....

....

....

HOW IT APPLIES TO MY LIFE:

Knowing this verse will be helpful when. . .

MY PRAYER FOR TODAY:

*Your Word have I hid in my heart,
that I may not sin against You.*
PSALM 119:11

Date: 2/21/22

MY MEMORY VERSE FOR TODAY: Psalm 100:1

Let the whole earth shout
triumphantly to the Lord
Psalms 100:1

This verse is important to remember because...

worship when we lift
up God is powerful
Make a joyful noise

WHAT IT MEANS TO MY FAITH:

the whole world should
worship God with praise

GO to my Room
when luke and brian
Push my Battung

Knowing this verse will be helpful when. . .

When luke Pushes
my buttons

MY PRAYER FOR TODAY:

GOD thank you for
creating me you are
worthy of all my praise
help me to honor you with
my life and to Glorey
you in everything i say and
do i want my life to her filld with
your
joy
amen

All the Holy Writings are God-given and are made
alive by Him. Man is helped when he is taught God's Word.
It shows what is wrong. It changes the way of a man's
life. It shows him how to be right with God. It gives
the man who belongs to God everything
he needs to work well for Him.

2 TIMOTHY 3:16–17

Date:

MY MEMORY VERSE FOR TODAY:

Rejoyce in the lord always
I Say It agian Rejoce

This verse is important to remember because. . .

beCase you must always
Rejoyc

WHAT IT MEANS TO MY FAITH:

It means that you
should always Rejoye

HOW IT APPLIES TO MY LIFE:

I must Rejoyce no
matter what

Knowing this verse will be helpful when. . .

When ever I am sad
and I need to
Regoyce

MY PRAYER FOR TODAY:

God you are more
important to me than
anything but somtimes
I live like I value the pra
of others more or
doing what I want to do
move thing you want me
to do please
help
me
live my
life
to please
niune truleh

But he finds joy in the Law of the Lord and thinks
about His Law day and night. This man is like a
tree planted by rivers of water, which gives its
fruit at the right time and its leaf never dries up.
Whatever he does will work out well for him.

PSALM 1:2-3

Date:

MY MEMORY VERSE FOR TODAY:

ie then you have been
raised with christ seek
the things above where
christ is seated at the Right
hant of God set your minds
on things above not on earth

This verse is important to remember because. . .

because I will
text and text

WHAT IT MEANS TO MY FAITH:

it means we should
be focast on God

HOW IT APPLIES TO MY LIFE:

When I am texting
I can stop

Knowing this verse will be helpful when. . .

When I am texting
and wont listen to
God

MY PRAYER FOR TODAY:

God I want to fecus
on the things that matter
the things that will ast
help me to look up today
to think about you to tatk
to you and tell others
about you in Jusesis
name amen

Your words became a joy to me and the
happiness of my heart. For I have been called
by Your name, O Lord God of All.
JEREMIAH 15:16

Date:

MY MEMORY VERSE FOR TODAY:

....

....

....

....

....

This verse is important to remember because. . .

....

....

....

....

....

WHAT IT MEANS TO MY FAITH:

....

....

....

....

....

HOW IT APPLIES TO MY LIFE:

Knowing this verse will be helpful when. . .

MY PRAYER FOR TODAY:

I have not turned away from the words of His lips.
I have stored up the words of His mouth.
They are worth more to me than the food I need.

JOB 23:12

Date:

MY MEMORY VERSE FOR TODAY:

....

....

....

....

....

This verse is important to remember because. . .

....

....

....

....

....

WHAT IT MEANS TO MY FAITH:

....

....

....

....

....

HOW IT APPLIES TO MY LIFE:

....

....

....

....

Knowing this verse will be helpful when. . .

....

....

....

....

....

MY PRAYER FOR TODAY:

....

....

....

....

"Keep these words in your heart that I am telling you today. . . . Talk about them when you sit in your house and when you walk on the road and when you lie down and when you get up. Tie them as something special to see on your hand and on your forehead. Write them beside the door of your house and on your gates."

DEUTERONOMY 6:6–9

Date:

MY MEMORY VERSE FOR TODAY:

....

....

....

....

....

This verse is important to remember because. . .

....

....

....

....

....

WHAT IT MEANS TO MY FAITH:

....

....

....

....

....

HOW IT APPLIES TO MY LIFE:

Knowing this verse will be helpful when. . .

MY PRAYER FOR TODAY:

"Those [seeds] which fell on good ground have heard the Word. They keep it in a good and true heart and they keep on giving good grain."

LUKE 8:15

Date:

MY MEMORY VERSE FOR TODAY:

....

....

....

....

....

This verse is important to remember because. . .

....

....

....

....

....

WHAT IT MEANS TO MY FAITH:

....

....

....

....

....

HOW IT APPLIES TO MY LIFE:

Knowing this verse will be helpful when. . .

MY PRAYER FOR TODAY:

*"Man lives by everything that comes
out of the mouth of the Lord."*
DEUTERONOMY 8:3

Date:

MY MEMORY VERSE FOR TODAY:

....

....

....

....

....

This verse is important to remember because. . .

....

....

....

....

....

....

WHAT IT MEANS TO MY FAITH:

....

....

....

....

....

Knowing this verse will be helpful when. . .

MY PRAYER FOR TODAY:

*Do not act like the sinful people of the world. Let God
change your life. First of all, let Him give you a new mind.
Then you will know what God wants you to do. And the
things you do will be good and pleasing and perfect.*

ROMANS 12:2

Date:

MY MEMORY VERSE FOR TODAY:

....

....

....

....

....

This verse is important to remember because. . .

....

....

....

....

....

WHAT IT MEANS TO MY FAITH:

....

....

....

....

....

....

....

....

....

Knowing this verse will be helpful when. . .

....

....

....

....

....

MY PRAYER FOR TODAY:

....

....

....

....

....

....

....

There is gold and many stones of great worth,
but the lips of much learning are worth more.
PROVERBS 20:15

Date:

MY MEMORY VERSE FOR TODAY:

This verse is important to remember because. . .

WHAT IT MEANS TO MY FAITH:

HOW IT APPLIES TO MY LIFE:

....

....

....

....

Knowing this verse will be helpful when. . .

....

....

....

....

....

MY PRAYER FOR TODAY:

....

....

....

....

*Anyone who hears the Word of God and does not obey
is like a man looking at his face in a mirror. After he sees
himself and goes away, he forgets what he looks like.
But the one who keeps looking into God's perfect Law
and does not forget it will do what it says and be
happy as he does it. God's Word makes men free.*

JAMES 1:23–25

Date:

MY MEMORY VERSE FOR TODAY:

....

....

....

....

....

This verse is important to remember because. . .

....

....

....

....

....

WHAT IT MEANS TO MY FAITH:

....

....

....

....

....

HOW IT APPLIES TO MY LIFE:

....

....

....

....

Knowing this verse will be helpful when. . .

....

....

....

....

....

MY PRAYER FOR TODAY:

....

....

....

....

....

....

*That is why we must listen all the more
to the truths we have been told. If we do not,
we may slip away from them.*
HEBREWS 2:1

Date:

MY MEMORY VERSE FOR TODAY:

....

....

....

....

....

This verse is important to remember because. . .

....

....

....

....

....

....

WHAT IT MEANS TO MY FAITH:

....

....

....

....

....

Knowing this verse will be helpful when. . .

MY PRAYER FOR TODAY:

Turn your ear and hear the words of the wise,
and open your mind to what they teach. For it will
be pleasing if you keep them in your heart,
so they may be ready on your lips.
PROVERBS 22:17–18

Date:

MY MEMORY VERSE FOR TODAY:

....

....

....

....

....

This verse is important to remember because. . .

....

....

....

....

....

....

WHAT IT MEANS TO MY FAITH:

....

....

....

....

....

....

....

....

....

Knowing this verse will be helpful when. . .

....

....

....

....

....

MY PRAYER FOR TODAY:

....

....

....

....

....

....

....

I will think about Your Law and
have respect for Your ways.
PSALM 119:15

Date:

MY MEMORY VERSE FOR TODAY:

....

....

....

....

....

This verse is important to remember because. . .

....

....

....

....

....

WHAT IT MEANS TO MY FAITH:

....

....

....

....

....

Knowing this verse will be helpful when. . .

MY PRAYER FOR TODAY:

"You will keep the man in perfect peace whose mind is kept on You, because he trusts in You."
ISAIAH 26:3

Date:

MY MEMORY VERSE FOR TODAY:

....

....

....

....

....

This verse is important to remember because. . .

....

....

....

....

....

WHAT IT MEANS TO MY FAITH:

....

....

....

....

....

Knowing this verse will be helpful when. . .

MY PRAYER FOR TODAY:

*God's Word is living and powerful. It is sharper than
a sword that cuts both ways. It cuts straight into where
the soul and spirit meet and it divides them. It cuts into
the joints and bones. It tells what the heart is
thinking about and what it wants to do.*

HEBREWS 4:12

Date:

MY MEMORY VERSE FOR TODAY:

....

....

....

....

....

This verse is important to remember because. . .

....

....

....

....

....

WHAT IT MEANS TO MY FAITH:

....

....

....

....

....

Knowing this verse will be helpful when. . .

MY PRAYER FOR TODAY:

*"Make them holy for Yourself by
the truth. Your Word is truth."*
JOHN 17:17

Date:

MY MEMORY VERSE FOR TODAY:

....

....

....

....

....

This verse is important to remember because. . .

....

....

....

....

....

....

WHAT IT MEANS TO MY FAITH:

....

....

....

....

....

HOW IT APPLIES TO MY LIFE:

....

....

....

....

Knowing this verse will be helpful when. . .

....

....

....

....

....

MY PRAYER FOR TODAY:

....

....

....

....

....

....

"Agree with God, and be at peace with Him. Then good will come to you. Receive the teaching from His mouth, and keep His words in your heart."

JOB 22:21–22

Date:

MY MEMORY VERSE FOR TODAY:

This verse is important to remember because. . .

WHAT IT MEANS TO MY FAITH:

HOW IT APPLIES TO MY LIFE:

....

....

....

....

Knowing this verse will be helpful when. . .

....

....

....

....

....

MY PRAYER FOR TODAY:

....

....

....

....

....

....

....

I will lift up my hands to Your Word,
which I love, and I will think about Your Law.
PSALM 119:48

Date:

MY MEMORY VERSE FOR TODAY:

....

....

....

....

....

This verse is important to remember because. . .

....

....

....

....

....

WHAT IT MEANS TO MY FAITH:

....

....

....

....

....

HOW IT APPLIES TO MY LIFE:

....

....

....

....

Knowing this verse will be helpful when. . .

....

....

....

....

....

MY PRAYER FOR TODAY:

....

....

....

....

....

Keep your minds thinking about whatever is true,
whatever is respected, whatever is right, whatever is pure,
whatever can be loved, and whatever is well thought of.
If there is anything good and worth giving thanks
for, think about these things.
PHILIPPIANS 4:8

Date:

MY MEMORY VERSE FOR TODAY:

....
....
....
....
....

This verse is important to remember because. . .

....
....
....
....
....
....

WHAT IT MEANS TO MY FAITH:

....
....
....
....
....

....

....

....

....

Knowing this verse will be helpful when. . .

....

....

....

....

....

MY PRAYER FOR TODAY:

....

....

....

....

....

....

....

*"Keep these words in your heart
that I am telling you today."*

DEUTERONOMY 6:6

Date:

MY MEMORY VERSE FOR TODAY:

....

....

....

....

....

This verse is important to remember because. . .

....

....

....

....

....

WHAT IT MEANS TO MY FAITH:

....

....

....

....

....

....

....

....

....

Knowing this verse will be helpful when. . .

....

....

....

....

....

MY PRAYER FOR TODAY:

....

....

....

....

....

....

Listen to my words. Turn your ear to my sayings.
Do not let them leave your eyes. Keep them
in the center of your heart.
PROVERBS 4:20–21

Date:

MY MEMORY VERSE FOR TODAY:

....

....

....

....

....

This verse is important to remember because. . .

....

....

....

....

....

....

WHAT IT MEANS TO MY FAITH:

....

....

....

....

....

....

....

....

....

Knowing this verse will be helpful when. . .

....

....

....

....

....

MY PRAYER FOR TODAY:

....

....

....

....

....

*Let the teaching of Christ and His words keep on living
in you. These make your lives rich and full of wisdom.
Keep on teaching and helping each other. Sing the Songs
of David and the church songs and the songs of
heaven with hearts full of thanks to God.*

COLOSSIANS 3:16

Date:

MY MEMORY VERSE FOR TODAY:

....

....

....

....

....

This verse is important to remember because. . .

....

....

....

....

....

....

WHAT IT MEANS TO MY FAITH:

....

....

....

....

....

HOW IT APPLIES TO MY LIFE:

....

....

....

....

Knowing this verse will be helpful when. . .

....

....

....

....

....

MY PRAYER FOR TODAY:

....

....

....

....

....

....

....

....

Your Word is a lamp to my feet and a light to my path.
PSALM 119:105

Date:

MY MEMORY VERSE FOR TODAY:

....

....

....

....

....

This verse is important to remember because. . .

....

....

....

....

....

WHAT IT MEANS TO MY FAITH:

....

....

....

....

....

HOW IT APPLIES TO MY LIFE:

....

....

....

....

Knowing this verse will be helpful when. . .

....

....

....

....

....

MY PRAYER FOR TODAY:

....

....

....

....

....

....

Do your best to know that God is pleased with you.
Be as a workman who has nothing to be ashamed
of. Teach the words of truth in the right way.
2 TIMOTHY 2:15

Date:

MY MEMORY VERSE FOR TODAY:

....

....

....

....

....

This verse is important to remember because. . .

....

....

....

....

....

WHAT IT MEANS TO MY FAITH:

....

....

....

....

....

Knowing this verse will be helpful when. . .

MY PRAYER FOR TODAY:

I will be glad in Your Law. I will not forget Your Word.
PSALM 119:16

Date:

MY MEMORY VERSE FOR TODAY:

....

....

....

....

....

This verse is important to remember because. . .

....

....

....

....

....

WHAT IT MEANS TO MY FAITH:

....

....

....

....

....

....

....

....

....

Knowing this verse will be helpful when. . .

....

....

....

....

....

MY PRAYER FOR TODAY:

....

....

....

....

....

....

"Keep these words of mine in your heart and in your soul.
Tie them as something special to see upon your hand
and on your forehead between your eyes."

DEUTERONOMY 11:18

Date:

MY MEMORY VERSE FOR TODAY:

....

....

....

....

....

This verse is important to remember because. . .

....

....

....

....

....

WHAT IT MEANS TO MY FAITH:

....

....

....

....

....

HOW IT APPLIES TO MY LIFE:

....

....

....

....

Knowing this verse will be helpful when. . .

....

....

....

....

....

MY PRAYER FOR TODAY:

....

....

....

....

....

....

....

....

Your Laws are wonderful, and so I obey them.
PSALM 119:129

Date:

MY MEMORY VERSE FOR TODAY:

....

....

....

....

....

This verse is important to remember because. . .

....

....

....

....

....

WHAT IT MEANS TO MY FAITH:

....

....

....

....

....

HOW IT APPLIES TO MY LIFE:

....

....

....

....

Knowing this verse will be helpful when. . .

....

....

....

....

....

MY PRAYER FOR TODAY:

....

....

....

....

....

....

Do not let kindness and truth leave you. Tie them around your neck. Write them upon your heart. So you will find favor and good understanding in the eyes of God and man.

PROVERBS 3:3–4

Date: _____

MY MEMORY VERSE FOR TODAY:

....
....
....
....
....

This verse is important to remember because. . .

....
....
....
....
....

WHAT IT MEANS TO MY FAITH:

....
....
....
....

....

....

....

....

Knowing this verse will be helpful when. . .

....

....

....

....

....

MY PRAYER FOR TODAY:

....

....

....

....

....

....

....

Those who love Your Law have great peace,
and nothing will cause them to be hurt in their spirit.
PSALM 119:165

Date:

MY MEMORY VERSE FOR TODAY:

....

....

....

....

....

This verse is important to remember because. . .

....

....

....

....

....

....

WHAT IT MEANS TO MY FAITH:

....

....

....

....

....

HOW IT APPLIES TO MY LIFE:

Knowing this verse will be helpful when. . .

MY PRAYER FOR TODAY:

*Do not forget my teaching. Let your heart keep
my words. For they will add to you many
days and years of life and peace.*
PROVERBS 3:1–2

Date:

MY MEMORY VERSE FOR TODAY:

....

....

....

....

....

This verse is important to remember because. . .

....

....

....

....

....

WHAT IT MEANS TO MY FAITH:

....

....

....

....

....

HOW IT APPLIES TO MY LIFE:

Knowing this verse will be helpful when. . .

MY PRAYER FOR TODAY:

*"And the Lord today has made it known that you
are His own people, as He promised you."*
DEUTERONOMY 26:18

Date:

MY MEMORY VERSE FOR TODAY:

....

....

....

....

....

This verse is important to remember because. . .

....

....

....

....

....

....

WHAT IT MEANS TO MY FAITH:

....

....

....

....

....

....

....

....

....

Knowing this verse will be helpful when. . .

....

....

....

....

....

MY PRAYER FOR TODAY:

....

....

....

....

....

....

*You have known the Holy Writings since you were a
child. They are able to give you wisdom that leads
to being saved from the punishment of sin
by putting your trust in Christ Jesus.*

2 TIMOTHY 3:15

Date:

MY MEMORY VERSE FOR TODAY:

....

....

....

....

....

This verse is important to remember because. . .

....

....

....

....

....

....

WHAT IT MEANS TO MY FAITH:

....

....

....

....

....

....

....

....

....

Knowing this verse will be helpful when. . .

....

....

....

....

....

MY PRAYER FOR TODAY:

....

....

....

....

....

....

*"This book of the Law must not leave your mouth.
Think about it day and night, so you may be careful
to do all that is written in it. Then all will go well
with you. You will receive many good things."*

JOSHUA 1:8

Date:

MY MEMORY VERSE FOR TODAY:

....

....

....

....

....

This verse is important to remember because. . .

....

....

....

....

....

....

WHAT IT MEANS TO MY FAITH:

....

....

....

....

....

HOW IT APPLIES TO MY LIFE:

Knowing this verse will be helpful when. . .

MY PRAYER FOR TODAY:

Trust in the Lord with all your heart, and do not trust in your own understanding. Agree with Him in all your ways, and He will make your paths straight.

PROVERBS 3:5–6

Date:

MY MEMORY VERSE FOR TODAY:

....

....

....

....

....

This verse is important to remember because. . .

....

....

....

....

....

WHAT IT MEANS TO MY FAITH:

....

....

....

....

....

Knowing this verse will be helpful when. . .

MY PRAYER FOR TODAY:

Do not worry. Learn to pray about everything.
Give thanks to God as you ask Him for what you need.
The peace of God is much greater than the human
mind can understand. This peace will keep your
hearts and minds through Christ Jesus.

PHILIPPIANS 4:6–7

Date:

MY MEMORY VERSE FOR TODAY:

....

....

....

....

....

This verse is important to remember because. . .

....

....

....

....

....

WHAT IT MEANS TO MY FAITH:

....

....

....

....

....

HOW IT APPLIES TO MY LIFE:

....

....

....

....

Knowing this verse will be helpful when. . .

....

....

....

....

....

MY PRAYER FOR TODAY:

....

....

....

....

....

....

....

"First of all, look for the holy nation of God. Be right with Him. All these other things will be given to you also."
MATTHEW 6:33

Date:

MY MEMORY VERSE FOR TODAY:

....

....

....

....

....

This verse is important to remember because. . .

....

....

....

....

....

WHAT IT MEANS TO MY FAITH:

....

....

....

....

....

....

....

....

....

Knowing this verse will be helpful when. . .

....

....

....

....

....

MY PRAYER FOR TODAY:

....

....

....

....

....

....

....

....

Look for the Lord and live.
AMOS 5:6

Date:

MY MEMORY VERSE FOR TODAY:

....

....

....

....

....

This verse is important to remember because. . .

....

....

....

....

....

....

WHAT IT MEANS TO MY FAITH:

....

....

....

....

....

Knowing this verse will be helpful when. . .

MY PRAYER FOR TODAY:

*"It is written, 'Man is not to live on bread only.
Man is to live by every word that God speaks.'"*
MATTHEW 4:4

Date:

MY MEMORY VERSE FOR TODAY:

....

....

....

....

....

This verse is important to remember because. . .

....

....

....

....

....

....

WHAT IT MEANS TO MY FAITH:

....

....

....

....

....

HOW IT APPLIES TO MY LIFE:

....
....
....
....

Knowing this verse will be helpful when. . .

....
....
....
....
....

MY PRAYER FOR TODAY:

....
....
....
....
....
....

"Be careful to listen to all these words I am telling you.
Then it will go well with you and your children after
you forever. For you will be doing what is good
and right in the eyes of the Lord your God."
DEUTERONOMY 12:28

Date:

MY MEMORY VERSE FOR TODAY:

This verse is important to remember because. . .

WHAT IT MEANS TO MY FAITH:

HOW IT APPLIES TO MY LIFE:

....

....

....

....

Knowing this verse will be helpful when. . .

....

....

....

....

....

MY PRAYER FOR TODAY:

....

....

....

....

....

....

....

*"Come here. Listen to the words
of the Lord your God."*
JOSHUA 3:9

Date:

MY MEMORY VERSE FOR TODAY:

....
....
....
....
....

This verse is important to remember because. . .

....
....
....
....
....

WHAT IT MEANS TO MY FAITH:

....
....
....
....
....

HOW IT APPLIES TO MY LIFE:

Knowing this verse will be helpful when. . .

MY PRAYER FOR TODAY:

*"Those who hear the Word of God
and obey it are happy."*
LUKE 11:28

Date:

MY MEMORY VERSE FOR TODAY:

....

....

....

....

....

This verse is important to remember because. . .

....

....

....

....

....

WHAT IT MEANS TO MY FAITH:

....

....

....

....

....

HOW IT APPLIES TO MY LIFE:

Knowing this verse will be helpful when. . .

MY PRAYER FOR TODAY:

*Tell them to put their faith in the teaching and the Law.
If they do not speak what this word says, it is
because they have no light in them.*

ISAIAH 8:20

Date:

MY MEMORY VERSE FOR TODAY:

....

....

....

....

....

This verse is important to remember because. . .

....

....

....

....

....

WHAT IT MEANS TO MY FAITH:

....

....

....

....

....

HOW IT APPLIES TO MY LIFE:

....
....
....
....

Knowing this verse will *be* helpful when. . .

....
....
....
....
....

MY PRAYER FOR TODAY:

....
....
....
....
....
....
....
....

"What the man plants is the Word of God."
MARK 4:14

Date:

MY MEMORY VERSE FOR TODAY:

....
....
....
....
....

This verse is important to remember because. . .

....
....
....
....
....
....

WHAT IT MEANS TO MY FAITH:

....
....
....
....
....

HOW IT APPLIES TO MY LIFE:

....

....

....

....

Knowing this verse will be helpful when. . .

....

....

....

....

....

MY PRAYER FOR TODAY:

....

....

....

....

....

....

But whoever obeys His Word has the love of
God made perfect in him. This is the way
to know if you belong to Christ.
1 JOHN 2:5

Date:

MY MEMORY VERSE FOR TODAY:

....

....

....

....

....

This verse is important to remember because. . .

....

....

....

....

....

....

WHAT IT MEANS TO MY FAITH:

....

....

....

....

....

HOW IT APPLIES TO MY LIFE:

Knowing this verse will be helpful when. . .

MY PRAYER FOR TODAY:

Loving God means to obey His Word,
and His Word is not hard to obey.
1 JOHN 5:3

Date:

MY MEMORY VERSE FOR TODAY:

....

....

....

....

....

This verse is important to remember because. . .

....

....

....

....

....

....

WHAT IT MEANS TO MY FAITH:

....

....

....

....

....

HOW IT APPLIES TO MY LIFE:

Knowing this verse will be helpful when. . .

MY PRAYER FOR TODAY:

*You have kept God's Word in your hearts.
You have power over the devil.*
1 JOHN 2:14

Date:

MY MEMORY VERSE FOR TODAY:

....

....

....

....

....

This verse is important to remember because. . .

....

....

....

....

....

WHAT IT MEANS TO MY FAITH:

....

....

....

....

....

HOW IT APPLIES TO MY LIFE:

Knowing this verse will be helpful when. . .

MY PRAYER FOR TODAY:

*This new life is from the Word
of God which lives forever.*
1 PETER 1:23

Date:

MY MEMORY VERSE FOR TODAY:

This verse is important to remember because. . .

WHAT IT MEANS TO MY FAITH:

....

....

....

....

Knowing this verse will be helpful when. . .

....

....

....

....

....

MY PRAYER FOR TODAY:

....

....

....

....

....

....

*Put out of your life all that is unclean and wrong.
Receive with a gentle spirit the Word that was taught.
It has the power to save your souls from
the punishment of sin.*

JAMES 1:21

Date:

MY MEMORY VERSE FOR TODAY:

....

....

....

....

....

This verse is important to remember because. . .

....

....

....

....

....

WHAT IT MEANS TO MY FAITH:

....

....

....

....

....

Knowing this verse will be helpful when. . .

MY PRAYER FOR TODAY:

Do you remember what God said to you when He called you His sons? "My son, listen when the Lord punishes you. Do not give up when He tells you what you must do."

HEBREWS 12:5

Date:

MY MEMORY VERSE FOR TODAY:

....

....

....

....

....

This verse is important to remember because. . .

....

....

....

....

....

WHAT IT MEANS TO MY FAITH:

....

....

....

....

....

HOW IT APPLIES TO MY LIFE:

....

....

....

....

Knowing this verse will be helpful when. . .

....

....

....

....

....

MY PRAYER FOR TODAY:

....

....

....

....

....

....

....

Remember your leaders who first spoke God's Word to you. Think of how they lived, and trust God as they did.
HEBREWS 13:7

Date:

MY MEMORY VERSE FOR TODAY:

....

....

....

....

....

This verse is important to remember because. . .

....

....

....

....

....

....

WHAT IT MEANS TO MY FAITH:

....

....

....

....

....

HOW IT APPLIES TO MY LIFE:

....

....

....

....

Knowing this verse will be helpful when. . .

....

....

....

....

....

MY PRAYER FOR TODAY:

....

....

....

....

....

....

....

*"I am happy to do Your will, O my God.
Your Law is within my heart."*
PSALM 40:8

Date:

MY MEMORY VERSE FOR TODAY:

....

....

....

....

....

This verse is important to remember because. . .

....

....

....

....

....

....

WHAT IT MEANS TO MY FAITH:

....

....

....

....

....

....

....

....

....

Knowing this verse will be helpful when. . .

....

....

....

....

....

MY PRAYER FOR TODAY:

....

....

....

....

....

....

....

....

The Word of God is not chained.
2 TIMOTHY 2:9

Date:

MY MEMORY VERSE FOR TODAY:

....

....

....

....

....

This verse is important to remember because. . .

....

....

....

....

....

....

WHAT IT MEANS TO MY FAITH:

....

....

....

....

....

....

....

....

....

Knowing this verse will be helpful when. . .

....

....

....

....

MY PRAYER FOR TODAY:

....

....

....

....

....

....

Everything God made is good. We should not put anything aside if we can take it and thank God for it. It is made holy by the Word of God and prayer.

1 TIMOTHY 4:4–5

Date:

MY MEMORY VERSE FOR TODAY:

....

....

....

....

....

This verse is important to remember because. . .

....

....

....

....

....

WHAT IT MEANS TO MY FAITH:

....

....

....

....

....

....

....

....

Knowing this verse will be helpful when. . .

....

....

....

....

....

MY PRAYER FOR TODAY:

....

....

....

....

....

....

*The Word of the Lord has been spoken by you in the
countries of Macedonia and Greece. People everywhere
know of your faith in God without our telling them.*
1 THESSALONIANS 1:8

Date:

MY MEMORY VERSE FOR TODAY:

....

....

....

....

....

This verse is important to remember because. . .

....

....

....

....

....

WHAT IT MEANS TO MY FAITH:

....

....

....

....

....

HOW IT APPLIES TO MY LIFE:

Knowing this verse will be helpful when. . .

MY PRAYER FOR TODAY:

*As for God, His way is perfect. The Word of the Lord
has stood the test. He is a covering for all
who go to Him for a safe place.*
PSALM 18:30

Date:

MY MEMORY VERSE FOR TODAY:

....

....

....

....

....

This verse is important to remember because. . .

....

....

....

....

....

....

WHAT IT MEANS TO MY FAITH:

....

....

....

....

....

HOW IT APPLIES TO MY LIFE:

Knowing this verse will be helpful when. . .

MY PRAYER FOR TODAY:

We always thank God that when you heard the Word of God from us, you believed it. You did not receive it as from men, but you received it as the Word of God. That is what it is. It is at work in the lives of you who believe.

1 THESSALONIANS 2:13

Date:

MY MEMORY VERSE FOR TODAY:

....

....

....

....

....

This verse is important to remember because. . .

....

....

....

....

....

WHAT IT MEANS TO MY FAITH:

....

....

....

....

....

HOW IT APPLIES TO MY LIFE:

....

....

....

....

Knowing this verse will be helpful when. . .

....

....

....

....

MY PRAYER FOR TODAY:

....

....

....

....

....

....

....

*Take the sword of the Spirit
which is the Word of God.*
EPHESIANS 6:17

Date:

MY MEMORY VERSE FOR TODAY:

....

....

....

....

....

This verse is important to remember because. . .

....

....

....

....

....

....

WHAT IT MEANS TO MY FAITH:

....

....

....

....

....

HOW IT APPLIES TO MY LIFE:

....

....

....

....

Knowing this verse will be helpful when. . .

....

....

....

....

....

MY PRAYER FOR TODAY:

....

....

....

....

....

....

We do not play with the Word of God or use it in a false way. Because we are telling the truth, we want men's hearts to listen to us. God knows our desires.

2 CORINTHIANS 4:2

Date:

MY MEMORY VERSE FOR TODAY:

....

....

....

....

....

This verse is important to remember because. . .

....

....

....

....

....

WHAT IT MEANS TO MY FAITH:

....

....

....

....

....

....

....

....

....

Knowing this verse will be helpful when. . .

....

....

....

....

....

MY PRAYER FOR TODAY:

....

....

....

....

....

....

....

Trust in the Lord with all your heart, and do
not trust in your own understanding.
PROVERBS 3:5

Date:

MY MEMORY VERSE FOR TODAY:

....

....

....

....

....

This verse is important to remember because. . .

....

....

....

....

....

WHAT IT MEANS TO MY FAITH:

....

....

....

....

....

Knowing this verse will be helpful when. . .

MY PRAYER FOR TODAY:

"Whoever is born of God listens to God's Word."
JOHN 8:47

Date:

MY MEMORY VERSE FOR TODAY:

....

....

....

....

....

This verse is important to remember because. . .

....

....

....

....

....

....

WHAT IT MEANS TO MY FAITH:

....

....

....

....

....

....

....

....

....

Knowing this verse will be helpful when. . .

....

....

....

....

....

MY PRAYER FOR TODAY:

....

....

....

....

....

....

....

....

"For God can do all things."
LUKE 1:37

Date:

MY MEMORY VERSE FOR TODAY:

....
....
....
....
....

This verse is important to remember because. . .

....
....
....
....
....
....

WHAT IT MEANS TO MY FAITH:

....
....
....
....
....

HOW IT APPLIES TO MY LIFE:

Knowing this verse will be helpful when. . .

MY PRAYER FOR TODAY:

*The grass dries up. The flower loses its color.
But the Word of our God stands forever.*
ISAIAH 40:8

Date:

MY MEMORY VERSE FOR TODAY:

....
....
....
....
....

This verse is important to remember because. . .

....
....
....
....
....
....

WHAT IT MEANS TO MY FAITH:

....
....
....
....
....

HOW IT APPLIES TO MY LIFE:

Knowing this verse will be helpful when. . .

MY PRAYER FOR TODAY:

*"You do read the Holy Writings. You think you
have life that lasts forever just because
you read them. They do tell of Me."*

JOHN 5:39

Date:

MY MEMORY VERSE FOR TODAY:

....

....

....

....

....

This verse is important to remember because. . .

....

....

....

....

....

....

WHAT IT MEANS TO MY FAITH:

....

....

....

....

....

Knowing this verse will be helpful when. . .

MY PRAYER FOR TODAY:

The man who reads this Book and listens to it
being read and obeys what it says will be happy.
For all these things will happen soon.

REVELATION 1:3

Date:

MY MEMORY VERSE FOR TODAY:

This verse is important to remember because. . .

WHAT IT MEANS TO MY FAITH:

HOW IT APPLIES TO MY LIFE:

....

....

....

....

Knowing this verse will be helpful when. . .

....

....

....

....

....

MY PRAYER FOR TODAY:

....

....

....

....

....

....

*The fear of the Lord is the beginning of
wisdom. All who obey His Laws have good
understanding. His praise lasts forever.*
PSALM 111:10

Date:

MY MEMORY VERSE FOR TODAY:

....

....

....

....

....

This verse is important to remember because. . .

....

....

....

....

....

WHAT IT MEANS TO MY FAITH:

....

....

....

....

....

HOW IT APPLIES TO MY LIFE:

....

....

....

....

Knowing this verse will be helpful when. . .

....

....

....

....

....

MY PRAYER FOR TODAY:

....

....

....

....

....

....

....

"You will know the truth and the truth will make you free."
JOHN 8:32

Date:

MY MEMORY VERSE FOR TODAY:

This verse is important to remember because. . .

WHAT IT MEANS TO MY FAITH:

HOW IT APPLIES TO MY LIFE:

Knowing this verse will be helpful when. . .

MY PRAYER FOR TODAY:

I will be glad in Your Law,
which I love.
PSALM 119:47

Date:

MY MEMORY VERSE FOR TODAY:

....

....

....

....

....

This verse is important to remember because. . .

....

....

....

....

....

WHAT IT MEANS TO MY FAITH:

....

....

....

....

....

....

....

....

....

Knowing this verse will be helpful when. . .

....

....

....

....

MY PRAYER FOR TODAY:

....

....

....

....

....

....

Happy is the man who finds wisdom, and the man
who gets understanding. For it is better
than getting silver and fine gold.
PROVERBS 3:13–14

Date:

MY MEMORY VERSE FOR TODAY:

....

....

....

....

....

This verse is important to remember because. . .

....

....

....

....

....

WHAT IT MEANS TO MY FAITH:

....

....

....

....

....

HOW IT APPLIES TO MY LIFE:

....

....

....

....

Knowing this verse will be helpful when. . .

....

....

....

....

....

MY PRAYER FOR TODAY:

....

....

....

....

....

....

....

"The Holy Writings you have just heard
have been completed today."
LUKE 4:21

Date:

MY MEMORY VERSE FOR TODAY:

....

....

....

....

....

This verse is important to remember because. . .

....

....

....

....

....

WHAT IT MEANS TO MY FAITH:

....

....

....

....

....

HOW IT APPLIES TO MY LIFE:

....

....

....

....

Knowing this verse will be helpful when. . .

....

....

....

....

....

MY PRAYER FOR TODAY:

....

....

....

....

....

....

....

*"But this has happened as the early preachers said
in the Holy Writings it would happen."*
MATTHEW 26:56

Date:

MY MEMORY VERSE FOR TODAY:

This verse is important to remember because. . .

WHAT IT MEANS TO MY FAITH:

HOW IT APPLIES TO MY LIFE:

Knowing this verse will be helpful when. . .

MY PRAYER FOR TODAY:

The earth is full of Your loving-kindness,
O Lord. Teach me Your Law.
PSALM 119:64

Date:

MY MEMORY VERSE FOR TODAY:

....

....

....

....

....

This verse is important to remember because. . .

....

....

....

....

....

WHAT IT MEANS TO MY FAITH:

....

....

....

....

....

HOW IT APPLIES TO MY LIFE:

....

....

....

Knowing this verse will be helpful when. . .

....

....

....

....

....

MY PRAYER FOR TODAY:

....

....

....

....

....

....

*As new babies want milk, you should want to drink the
pure milk which is God's Word so you will grow up
and be saved from the punishment of sin.*

1 PETER 2:2

Date:

MY MEMORY VERSE FOR TODAY:

....

....

....

....

....

This verse is important to remember because. . .

....

....

....

....

....

WHAT IT MEANS TO MY FAITH:

....

....

....

....

....

HOW IT APPLIES TO MY LIFE:

....

....

....

....

Knowing this verse will be helpful when. . .

....

....

....

....

....

MY PRAYER FOR TODAY:

....

....

....

....

....

....

....

First of all, I taught you what I had received. It was this:
Christ died for our sins as the Holy Writings said He would.
1 CORINTHIANS 15:3

MY MEMORY VERSE FOR TODAY:

This verse is important to remember because. . .

WHAT IT MEANS TO MY FAITH:

Knowing this verse will be helpful when. . .

MY PRAYER FOR TODAY:

*I am under an agreement with You, O God. I will give
You gifts of thanks. For You have set my soul free
from death. You have kept my feet from falling,
so I may walk with God in the light of life.*
PSALM 56:12–13

MY MEMORY VERSE FOR TODAY:

....

....

....

....

....

This verse is important to remember because. . .

....

....

....

....

....

WHAT IT MEANS TO MY FAITH:

....

....

....

....

....

HOW IT APPLIES TO MY LIFE:

....

....

....

....

Knowing this verse will be helpful when. . .

....

....

....

....

....

MY PRAYER FOR TODAY:

....

....

....

....

....

....

....

*"If you get your life from Me and My Words live in you,
ask whatever you want. It will be done for you."*

JOHN 15:7

Date:

MY MEMORY VERSE FOR TODAY:

....
....
....
....
....

This verse is important to remember because. . .

....
....
....
....
....

WHAT IT MEANS TO MY FAITH:

....
....
....
....
....

HOW IT APPLIES TO MY LIFE:

....

....

....

....

Knowing this verse will be helpful when. . .

....

....

....

....

....

MY PRAYER FOR TODAY:

....

....

....

....

....

....

....

The Law of his God is in his heart.
His steps do not leave it.
PSALM 37:31

Date:

MY MEMORY VERSE FOR TODAY:

....

....

....

....

....

This verse is important to remember because. . .

....

....

....

....

....

WHAT IT MEANS TO MY FAITH:

....

....

....

....

....

HOW IT APPLIES TO MY LIFE:

....

....

....

....

Knowing this verse will be helpful when. . .

....

....

....

....

....

MY PRAYER FOR TODAY:

....

....

....

....

....

....

....

*Obey the Word of God. If you hear only and do
not act, you are only fooling yourself.*
JAMES 1:22

Date:

MY MEMORY VERSE FOR TODAY:

....

....

....

....

....

This verse is important to remember because. . .

....

....

....

....

....

WHAT IT MEANS TO MY FAITH:

....

....

....

....

....

HOW IT APPLIES TO MY LIFE:

....

....

....

....

Knowing this verse will be helpful when. . .

....

....

....

....

....

MY PRAYER FOR TODAY:

....

....

....

....

....

....

*Everything that was written in the Holy Writings long
ago was written to teach us. By not giving up,
God's Word gives us strength and hope.*

ROMANS 15:4

Date:

MY MEMORY VERSE FOR TODAY:

....

....

....

....

....

This verse is important to remember because. . .

....

....

....

....

....

WHAT IT MEANS TO MY FAITH:

....

....

....

....

....

HOW IT APPLIES TO MY LIFE:

....

....

....

....

Knowing this verse will be helpful when. . .

....

....

....

....

....

MY PRAYER FOR TODAY:

....

....

....

....

....

....

*No part of the Holy Writings was ever made up by any
man. No part of the Holy Writings came long ago because
of what man wanted to write. But holy men who belonged
to God spoke what the Holy Spirit told them.*

2 PETER 1:20–21

Date:

MY MEMORY VERSE FOR TODAY:

This verse is important to remember because. . .

WHAT IT MEANS TO MY FAITH:

....

....

....

....

Knowing this verse will be helpful when. . .

....

....

....

....

....

MY PRAYER FOR TODAY:

....

....

....

....

....

....

The Lord will send His loving-kindness in the day.
And His song will be with me in the night,
a prayer to the God of my life.
PSALM 42:8

Date:

MY MEMORY VERSE FOR TODAY:

....
....
....
....
....

This verse is important to remember because. . .

....
....
....
....
....

WHAT IT MEANS TO MY FAITH:

....
....
....
....
....

HOW IT APPLIES TO MY LIFE:

....

....

....

....

Knowing this verse will be helpful when. . .

....

....

....

....

....

MY PRAYER FOR TODAY:

....

....

....

....

....

....

....

*Every word of God has been proven true. He is a
safe-covering to those who trust in Him.*

PROVERBS 30:5

Great Scriptures to Memorize!

Don't know where to begin with your scripture memorization? Check out the following suggested memory verses.

1. Genesis 1:27
2. Exodus 14:14
3. Leviticus 19:18
4. Numbers 23:19
5. Deuteronomy 6:4–5
6. Joshua 1:8
7. Judges 3:9
8. Ruth 2:12
9. 1 Samuel 16:7
10. 2 Samuel 7:22
11. 1 Kings 2:3
12. 2 Kings 20:5
13. 1 Chronicles 16:11
14. 1 Chronicles 29:17
15. 2 Chronicles 7:14
16. 2 Chronicles 12:14
17. 2 Chronicles 15:7
18. Ezra 8:22

42. Jeremiah 29:13

43. Jeremiah 32:17

44. Jeremiah 33:3

45. Lamentations 3:32–33

46. Ezekiel 36:27

47. Daniel 12:3

48. Hosea 14:9

49. Joel 2:23

50. Amos 5:14

51. Obadiah 1:15

52. Jonah 2:9

53. Micah 6:8

54. Nahum 1:7

55. Habakkuk 3:17–18

56. Zephaniah 3:17

57. Haggai 1:5

58. Zechariah 14:9

59. Malachi 3:6

60. Matthew 4:19

61. Matthew 5:16

62. Matthew 5:42

63. Matthew 6:9–13

64. Matthew 6:19–21

You'll Love These Other Books for Praying Girls!

The Prayer Map for Girls

This unique prayer journal is a fun and creative way for you to understand the importance and experience the power of prayer. Each page features a fun, 2-color design that guides you to write out specific thoughts, ideas, and lists. . . which then creates a specific "map" for you to follow as you talk to God.

Spiral Bound / 978-1-68322-559-1 / $7.99

3-Minute Prayers for Girls

You'll be encouraged to take a few moments of your day to pause, reflect, and renew your spirit with these 3-minute prayers. Each day's reading includes. . .

Minute 1: meditate on a brief scripture selection

Minute 2: pray, using the provided prayer to jump-start a conversation with God

Minute 3: reflect on a question for further thought

Just 3 short minutes, and you'll be on your way to delightful one-on-one time with the heavenly Father!

Paperback / 978-1-68322-885-1 / $4.99

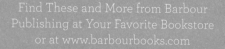